BABY'S BLUES

Tammy Ryan

BROADWAY PLAY PUBLISHING INC
New York
www.broadwayplaypublishing.com
info@broadwayplaypublishing.com

BABY'S BLUES
© Copyright 2006 by Tammy Ryan

1st printing: Nov 2006; 2nd printing Sept 2010
I S B N: 978-0-88145-316-4

Book design: Marie Donovan
Word processing: Microsoft Word
Typographic controls: Ventura Publisher
Typeface: Palatino
Printed and bound in the U S A

The first production of BABY'S BLUES was performed at The Pittsburgh Playhouse by The Rep, the professional theater company of Point Park University (Ronald Allan-Lindblom, Artistic Producing Director) opening on 27 October 2005. The cast and creative contributors were:

SUSAN ....Melanie Julian
MARCÉ .... Greg Longenhagen
GRANDMA .... Barbara Burney
GIRL ....Chesley Shannon
DOCTOR ....Eve Amplas
DAVID .... Paul Ford, Jr
TERRI ....Janelle Baker

Director .... Sheila McKenna
Set & costume design .... Pei-Chi Su
Lighting design ....Jennifer Ford, PhD
Sound design .... Elizabeth Atkinson
Doll design .... Tavia LaFollette
Production stage manager .... Kim Martin

CHARACTERS

SUSAN, *mid thirties first time mother*
MARCÉ, *a French nineteenth century physician, mid thirties*
GRANDMA, SUSAN's *mother, early sixties, lives in Florida*
GIRL, SUSAN's *ten year-old self, (actress in her twenties who can play ten)*
DOCTOR, *female, pediatrician in her early thirties*
DAVID, SUSAN's *husband, late thirties*
TERRI, SUSAN's *co-worker and best friend, late thirties*

Note on Characters: MARCÉ, GRANDMA *and* GIRL *are parts of* SUSAN's *inner world representing different aspects of her psyche and seen only by* SUSAN. *The* DOCTOR, DAVID *and* TERRI *exist in the outside reality.*

The character of MARCÉ *was inspired by* LOUIS VICTOR MARCÉ (1828-1864). *A 19th century French physician who in 1858 published a work entitled,* Treatise on the insanity of pregnant, newly delivered and nursing mothers.
The authority on post-partum illness for a hundred years, MARCÉ *was the first to sense that it was an organic illness. Later his work would be misquoted to prove the opposite, that post-partum depression and psychosis do not differ from depression and psychosis at any other time in a woman's life. The subject continues to be debated.*

NOTES FOR PRODUCTION

Scenes should move swiftly without breaks, frequent
blackouts, or intermission. Don't feel the need for
realism. For example, baby bathtub can be enormous.
The monitor can turn on and off by itself. Rely on lights
and especially sound, i.e. water rushing in tub, the roar
of static from baby monitor, surreal baby sounds, etc.
Sound functions as another character in the play,
revealing SUSAN's inner world while at the same time
pushing the action forward.

The baby itself can be represented in a variety of ways,
however, it should be obvious the baby is *not real*, and
is blatantly a doll, puppet, or whatever. In the first
production, the babies were represented by a series of
dolls wrapped in silk like material. At the start of the
play, when SUSAN gives birth, a scarlet scarf was pulled
out of her. The first baby was wrapped in this scarlet
material; each subsequent baby gradually went from
scarlet to pink to white by the end of the play. This, is
one solution.

With regard to the set, non-naturalistic works best,
although as with real babies, lots of props come into
play. The set design should facilitate the revelation
(and storage) of these, as well as quick transformations
from scene to scene. The original production was
played in the round, literally enclosing the audience
inside SUSAN's point of view. However it's staged,
the production's design should create opportunities
for surprises and facilitate the shifting reality.

for Devan and Dallas

PROLOGUE

(At rise: In dim light, a very pregnant woman rocks slowly back and forth establishing a rhythm that doesn't break except where indicated. Before we see her clearly, we hear her voice as if hearing her thoughts running like a stream of water. Her entire speech should be taped, until indicated otherwise. She is writing in a journal)

SUSAN: *(Voiceover)* Someone else's dream. That's it. I feel like I am dreaming someone else's dream. Is that the baby? That tenacious octopus floating warm and silent inside me, refusing to come out after *forty-two weeks*. Dreaming? *(Stops rocking, groaning, as baby moves inside)* An ocean rolling, a tsnuami starting on the other side of the world...ending...here. *(Starts rocking)* This is claustrophobic. This feeling. Like I can't get out. Is that me? Or the baby? *(Pause)* Try to think. I can't get out of what's coming up ahead. It's inevitable: "how-is-she-going-to-get-out?" Either, she's going to push, tear, grind her way out, down there, cracking my bones apart as she goes, emptying me out. Like shit. *(Beat)* I hope that doesn't happen. *(Beat)* But it's natural, isn't it? That's Nature. The life force. Squeezing me inside out like a ripe peach. Or, if something goes wrong, someone is going to, oh god, more fruit metaphors, split me open like a cantaloupe— *(Stops rocking, staring at walls)* I hate this wallpaper. Whose idea was this wallpaper? The color is making me sick. The baby is going to take one look at that wallpaper and start screaming. What was I thinking, yellow wallpaper? Why didn't I paint it a bright happy color like lilac? How long would it take to rip it down and start over?

(She is standing looking at wall, then) Where is my bliss?
I was supposed to be so fucking *happy*. I *never glowed*.
What bullshit. I hate being pregnant. It's like being held
hostage. All you can think is when, when am I going to
be free again? *(Softening, relaxing during the following)*
Although I did have that dream. I need to remember it.
(Back to rocking chair, writing in journal) The most
amazing technicolor dream. Bright pink naked, my
huge belly in front of me, I stepped into an icy pool
of aquamarine. My mother, of all people, was already
in the pool, as I watched my thighs immersed bright
pink under the absolute clarity of that water. Another
woman, my grandmother, in the pool, too. And a little
farther off, there were more women, smaller and
darker, dotting the way toward an open sea. I smiled at
my mother but she wasn't looking at me, she was facing
the other way— *(Suddenly tender, touching her belly,
tearing up)* Little fish. When it's your turn, I will smile
at you, I promise. Please God, let her be all right. Yes,
when the baby gets here, when it gets out, I'll be better
then. *(Suddenly the sound of something elastic breaking, like
a "pong")* Uhn. *(Speaking for the first time: surprised and
confused)* ...I'm all wet. *(Dawning on her what this means,
the voiced thoughts continue)* Oh no, oh no, oh no, not yet,
I take it back, I take it all back, I'm not ready, I didn't
finish my *Lamaze* class, I don't know what to do, I'm
not ready— *(She stands up, dropping journal and pen, then
suddenly doubles over with a contraction, when it passes,
she screams out loud.)* Daaaviiid!!

*(Lights black out on scream, in the transition the sounds of
her labor, with words woven in, spoken apart, like the taped
thoughts.)*

VOICED THOUGHTS: I am turning something pressing
black space I am disappearing into. I can't. I am not.
I am pressing into black opening up. I am falling.
Out of myself.

(The labor sounds climax, with the dissonant notes of a twisted lullaby in the darkness.)

Scene One

(The sound of running water. She is in a hospital bed. She wakes up and sees, sitting in the only chair in the room in the corner, a small man in his early thirties. He is dressed like a nineteenth century physician. He speaks French [translation on page 66])

MARCÉ: *Bonjour, Madame. Comment vous sentez-vous? Non ne parlez pas. Restez couchée, vous avez fourni un gros effort ce soir. Reposez-vous quand il est encore temps.*

SUSAN: I left the water running in the sink.

MARCÉ: *(Frowning slightly, touches her forehead, clucks his tongue) Legère fièvre, une sueur épaisse couvre le visage. Le visage est pâle, enflé, l'expression hébétée, le pouls est rapides, dites ahhh, (He sticks his tongue out, she imitates him) La langue est chargée, je peux? (He begins to palpate her uterus) L'utérus est hypertrophié, tendre, oui, mais retrouvera sa forme normale. Je recommande le sommeil. Et de longs bains chauds, le temps se chargera du reste. Y a-t-il quelqu'un qui puisse vous persuader de prendre soin de vous?*

SUSAN: I don't speak french.

MARCÉ: *(In heavily accented English)* We must ask the question: what is the connection between the uterus and the mind?

(MARCÉ exits. The ten year old GIRL enters from a corner and sits in the seat MARCÉ vacated. Right behind her, is GRANDMA pushing the cart with the baby on it. GRANDMA picks up the swaddled infant and starts patting its bottom. The girl cracks open a can of ginger ale. SUSAN sits up.)

Scene Two

GRANDMA: *(In a thick Brooklyn/Queens accent)* Then I noticed these little "stawks" which I'd never noticed before, running up and down the beach on these skinny little legs. I don't know why I never noticed them before, cause there were packs of them running up and down the beach. Egrits, I think they call em. They are so cute. *(To baby)* And so are you. There you go, back in your little casserole dish.

(AS soon as GRANDMA puts down the baby, the GIRL runs to the cart, peering at baby)

GIRL: *(Under their exchange)* Can I hold her?

SUSAN: What are you talking about?

GIRL: Can I hold her?

GRANDMA: Stawks. Little teeny stawks with skinny legs.

GIRL: Can I hold her?

SUSAN: Stalks? What are they—like plants?

GIRL: Let me hold her.

GRANDMA: *No! Stawks, stawks,* what's the matter with you, *(Giving the GIRL a look)* the birds that bring the babies.

SUSAN: You mean, stork?

GIRL: She means sex. *(Snorkeling in her gingerale)*

GRANDMA: You don't know about that and stop drinking soda, you'll get fat. *(To SUSAN)* They're called egrits.

SUSAN: I thought you weren't coming.

GRANDMA: *(To the baby)* Ah well, you'll survive, just like we all survived what our poor mothers did to us.

SUSAN: What does that mean?

GRANDMA: Oh you know, all the mistakes you're gonna make. She'll overcome it, just like we did.

SUSAN: We did.

GRANDMA: Yes we did. And you will too, my little dorito.

GIRL: Burrito! The nurse said she looked like a little burrito, not dorito. *(Looks at* SUSAN *like, isn't* GRANDMA *crazy!?)*

GRANDMA: Just so long as we don't put you in the oven by mistake. *(Looks at* SUSAN*)* How are you feeling?

SUSAN: I haven't taken a shower or bowel movement in forty-eight hours, I have a headache, my stitches hurt and I feel like I am falling off the edge of the world.

GRANDMA: Where is that doctor? Has anybody come to check you out?

SUSAN: She wants me to nurse her.

GRANDMA: The nurse came?

SUSAN: No, the pediatrician, she was here before you-showed up. She wants me to breastfeed.

GIRL: Ew.

GRANDMA: You're not gonna.

SUSAN: I don't know. It hurt.

GRANDMA: It's *barbaric.*

SUSAN: It's supposed to be best for the baby.

GRANDMA: So is living in the Taj Mahal. I didn't "breastfeed" you and you survived. Besides she liked her bottle just fine.

SUSAN: You gave her a bottle?

GRANDMA: You were sleeping when I came in; she was hungry and she sucked it right down.

(Before SUSAN *can protest, the* DOCTOR *enters. She is about the same age as* SUSAN, *mid-thirties, polite but reserved, professional, but not cold)*

DOCTOR: *(To* SUSAN*)* Morning, Mom. How are we feeling?

SUSAN: Hi.

GRANDMA: Finally.

DOCTOR: I checked the baby when she was in the nursery.

SUSAN: Is she all right?

DOCTOR: She's fine. You make good babies. And how's Mom doing?

SUSAN: She's a little tired.

DOCTOR: Bet you feel like you ran the marathon. Hahaha. I noticed, in the nursery, it said you were bottlefeeding.

SUSAN: Did it?

DOCTOR: Could I convince you to breastfeed instead?

GRANDMA: I don't think so.

(Pause)

SUSAN: I don't think I could.

DOCTOR: We could make it work.

GRANDMA: *(Snorting) We.*

DOCTOR: Unless you feel strongly about it, I would urge you to try breastfeeding, even for a few weeks, it's best for baby.

GRANDMA: I raised six kids on corn syrup and evaporated milk I boiled right on the stove and they turned out all right.

SUSAN: I tried, I couldn't do it.

DOCTOR: You haven't given it a chance. But you want to do what's comfortable for you.

GRANDMA: It's gonna be hard enough without adding that.

SUSAN: I'm feeling a little overwhelmed at the moment.

DOCTOR: Sure.

GRANDMA: Do you have children?

DOCTOR: *(Writing down,* SUSAN*'s "answer")* No.

GRANDMA: Didn't think so.

DOCTOR: Is there someone to help you?

GRANDMA: I live in Florida now and I love it. I lived all my life in New York, but then I couldn't take the winters no more. Of course I wanted to see the baby. But I can't be cold anymore. She has a husband. Let him help her. After all he had something to do with this.

DOCTOR: When you get home?

GIRL: I'll help her.

SUSAN: My husband.

DOCTOR: Good.

SUSAN: He had to go buy a car seat. She was a little early; we weren't ready....

GRANDMA: Last minute Davey.

DOCTOR: I understand. But he will be here to take you home? Because you'll need help in the beginning. You'll get a brochure that explains all this when they release you, but I can tell you, you should stay off your feet as much as possible, get as much rest as you can. Let others do the household chores, cook dinner, do the laundry. You only take care of your baby and yourself. If you have any questions don't hesitate to call. Even stupid questions. Hahaha. That's what we're here for.

SUSAN: Thank you.

DOCTOR: Beautiful baby. You did a good job.

GRANDMA: Little dorito is perfect.

SUSAN: *(Tearing up)* Thank you.

DOCTOR: *(Not unsympathetic)* Now comes the hard part.

(DAVID, SUSAN's husband enters. He is harried but exhilarated. He is carrying bags of food and a carseat)

DOCTOR: Oh Good, Congratulations, Dad. The two of you make good babies. Have more. Hahahaha.

(GIRL sneaks another can of gingerale from Susan's tray)

GRANDMA: You're gonna rot out your teeth.

DAVID: If I can survive her having them. She sucker punched me in the delivery room.

SUSAN: Are you still mad about that?

DAVID: I told you I'm not mad. It just wasn't what I was expecting at that moment. "Okay, honey, you're ready to push:" *pow*.

GRANDMA: You don't want to antagonize him, you're gonna need his help.

DOCTOR: Transition's always pretty tricky. If they had guns in the delivery room there'd be a lot of dead husbands. Hahaha. And maybe a few less obstetricians. That's why pediatricians stay out of the delivery room. Hahahaha. We only deal with the end product, not the process. Hahaha. Take good care of that baby. See you in two weeks. Unless, of course, we need to see her sooner.

(She exits.)

GRANDMA: Product. Like she's a box of cereal. *(Eyes DAVID)* My husband, blind drunk in some bar during the event, always arrived at the hospital with flowers.

DAVID: I know my wife, *(Kisses her)* she wants food.

SUSAN: I'm not hungry.

GIRL: I am.

GRANDMA: I'll just pick at whatever you brought.

DAVID: How about a smile?

SUSAN: How about it?

(Baby suddenly starts crying. It's a horrible sound, goes right through you. They all look at the baby, then at SUSAN. GRANDMA starts eating, GIRL joins her)

DAVID: What do we do?

GRANDMA: Breast*feed* her. Hahahahaha. *(Gnawing on chicken leg)* Pick her up. She's your baby.

(SUSAN, tentatively, terrified, picks the baby up like a bundle of fragile glass)

DAVID: Watch her neck!

SUSAN: I am!

(SUSAN holds the baby, who continues to cry. They all watch her. SUSAN looks to them for guidance. There is nothing but chewing from GRANDMA. The GIRL stands up as if to help but doesn't move. DAVID knows this is not his call. Then the GIRL opens drawer under baby's glass bed, pulls out bottle. She hands it to SUSAN who puts it in baby's mouth. Immediate quiet.)

GRANDMA: Good girl.

(GRANDMA *and* GIRL *polish off wings.* DAVID *stands awkwardly, not sure what his role is.* SUSAN *looks like she is feeding the baby poison, but the baby is indeed "sucking it down."* SUSAN *holds up empty bottle.*)

SUSAN: That was too fast.

(Baby starts wailing again)

GRANDMA: *(Mouth full)* Burp 'er.

SUSAN: What?

(GIRL belches)

GRANDMA: Burp her. Hahahaha.

DAVID: Let me see if I can catch the doctor. *(Exits)*

(SUSAN *puts baby to her shoulder and very lightly pats her back)*

GRANDMA: Oh for godsake.

(GRANDMA *wipes her hands, takes baby, throws her against her shoulder and whacks her three times.* GIRL *watches as she finishes eating, etc. Baby burps. All of* SUSAN'*s confidence crumbles in this moment)*

GRANDMA: See.

(GRANDMA *hands baby back to* SUSAN *who looks pale)*

GRANDMA: What's the matter with you? *(Touches her forehead)* You're all clammy.

GIRL: Is she sick?

GRANDMA: She just had a baby. Her organs are re-adjusting. She'll be fine.

(DAVID returns)

DAVID: I couldn't find her. Oh, she's quiet.

SUSAN: *(Smiling with relief)* She's sleeping.

DAVID: You look like a natural Mother already.

SUSAN: Yeah?

GRANDMA: Put her down; don't want to spoil her.

DAVID: She seems to sleep a lot.

GRANDMA: Don't get used to it.

DAVID: Oh! I almost forgot. Your Mom sent this. *(Hands her a wrapped package, and begins packing up everything)*

GRANDMA: Nothin big. I know how you like to write in your diary.

SUSAN: Oh...it's a journal...how pretty.

GRANDMA: It's a baby diary, so you can write everything down when it happens so you don't forget. And no one can accuse you of anything that didn't happen later.

(DAVID with his arms full of flowers and baby things)

DAVID: I'm gonna start loading up the car with some of this stuff now, so everything will be set up for you when you get home. I'll be right back. *(He exits, then quickly returns.)* I love you. *(He kisses her, then)* Are you sure about not breastfeeding? *(At the look on her face)* Okay, then I'm gonna take some of this formula. This shit is expensive. But whatever you want to do, is okay by me. I'll be back. *(Kisses her again, then runs out)*

SUSAN: *(Tearing up again; to GRANDMA)* I wish you were really here.

GRANDMA: *(Tearing up too)* My baby.

GIRL: Can I hold her now?

(A woman enters with flowers and baby balloons and a bright yellow gift bag)

TERRI: Susan?

(GRANDMA and GIRL exit.)

SUSAN: Terri.

TERRI: I saw David going down the hall with all those flowers! Here's some more! Hey Suze, are you crying?

SUSAN: No, no, no.

TERRI: Hey you just had a baby, cry if you want to.

SUSAN: It was nice of you to visit.

TERRI: My best friend just had a baby, of course I'm going to visit— Oh my gosh, Susan she is beautiful. I can't believe you had a baby!

SUSAN: Me neither.

TERRI: Are you so happy you can't stand it?

SUSAN: That's right.

TERRI: Everybody says congratulations. *(Peering at baby in SUSAN's arms)* Oh my, Susan. How are you ever going to go back to work with this precious little thing at home? So, how was labour? Was it horrible?

SUSAN: I don't have the words for it.

TERRI: Is it true what they say, you forget?

SUSAN: I don't—feel right, Terri.

TERRI: *(Looks at her a moment, then)* You just had a baby! Give yourself a chance to recover!

SUSAN: I never had a baby before. I don't know what to do!

TERRI: Don't worry when you get home, your maternal instinct will kick in. Hey, call me, I'll come over on weekends, I mean it. I'll get my baby fix and you can take a nap or whatever. Since it doesn't look like there are any babies on my horizon. A man is usually required. That's all right. Can I hold her?

SUSAN: Sure.

(SUSAN *passes her the baby*)

TERRI: She's so light. Like a bag of feathers. Oh, look at the tiny fingernails. (*Referring to yellow bag*) That's for you, since I missed the shower. If you already have one I can return it. It's a baby monitor, of course you have one, I can bring it back. What do you need, I'll get you whatever you need.

SUSAN: I don't know what I need.

TERRI: I'll return it.

SUSAN: No, no, no, that's okay. I'm sure I can always use another one, thank you, Terri.

TERRI: (*Gently handing her back the baby*) This way Mama will hear you no matter where she is in the house. I'm so happy for you. You're a mother now.

(TERRI's *Words "You're a mother now" have a strange hollow, echoey sound. The wind picks up*)

SUSAN: Is it snowing outside?

TERRI: It was starting to. Flurries. Nothing to worry about. (*"Nothing to worry about" has the echoey sound*)

SUSAN: (*To baby*) Nothing to worry about.

(*Fade to black*)

Scene Three

(*Home from the hospital. A raging snowstorm and howling wind outside.* SUSAN *swaddles and re-swaddles the baby throughout scene*)

DAVID: (*Enters with more flowers and diapers*) That's it; that's everything. How is she? (*Looking over* SUSAN's *shoulder at baby*) ...And on the day we brought you home from the hospital it was snowing like a bastard...

SUSAN: David.

DAVID: What? She doesn't understand.

SUSAN: I can't get this. I don't know how she did it. This isn't right.

DAVID: It looks okay.

SUSAN: No, look, it's falling off. It was tight in the hospital. The nurse had her wrapped like a little package.

DAVID: She's not going to know the difference.

SUSAN: They say to keep the baby "swaddled" for a reason. Swaddled not tossed together like a salad.

DAVID: What?

SUSAN: It makes them feel safe.

DAVID: Okay let me do it.

(He unswaddles baby, which rolls across the couch. SUSAN winces, he holds baby in one hand and folds blanket like a napkin under her, then places baby squarely on blanket, wrapping quickly)

SUSAN: Safe, David, safe! How is that making her feel safe—?

DAVID: There. Swaddled. *(Hands baby to SUSAN)* I wish someone would swaddle me.

(He tries to hug SUSAN who shrugs him off.)

SUSAN: Six weeks buddy.

DAVID: I was just going to give you a hug. You look like you could use one. Come on, sit down, let's relax.

SUSAN: I don't think I'll ever relax again.

DAVID: Of course you will, stop being such a drama queen, Suze. Come on, be happy.

SUSAN: I'd be happy if I could put her in a desk drawer, close the drawer and be done for now. I'll take her out later. When I can think straight.

DAVID: She's not the monthly project report.

SUSAN: Then I'd know what to do with her.

DAVID: She's beautiful.

SUSAN: She is. *(Beat)* But what are we going to do?

DAVID: What do you mean?

SUSAN: Next. Should we sit here, should we put her in the bassinet, or the crib, or just hold her? Should we stay up and wait for her to get hungry, or should we go to bed?

DAVID: I say let's go to bed. I'm beat.

SUSAN: But what if she cries?

DAVID: Then we'll wake up.

SUSAN: I think I want to do something else.

DAVID: Okay. How about something to eat?

SUSAN: How about we put something together.

DAVID: Ohhh-kayyy. How about this: The baby monitors. This way, if she cries in the middle of the night. We'll hear her.

SUSAN: What's to put together, all you have to do is plug them in. I'm looking for a project, David, so I can feel like we got something done.

DAVID: I got news for you: everything related to babies is a project. In the past forty-eight hours, I put together a crib, a bassinet, a bouncy chair and a car seat, and I've learned the hard way to read the instructions *first*.

SUSAN: So now that I'm a mother, I'm an idiot.

DAVID: No. Where did you get that from? I just want to read the instructions so I don't screw up. You just hold your baby. And practice relaxing.

SUSAN: Yeah, how do I do that? She didn't come with instructions.

DAVID: She's the only thing that doesn't.

SUSAN: Well, she should.

(DAVID *unpacks baby monitors, starts reading.* SUSAN *is quiet, staring at the wreck of the house*)

DAVID: Simple enough.

SUSAN: What have you been doing here the last couple of days? Having wild parties?

DAVID: Yeah, that's right, wild bachelor parties.

SUSAN: Everything is all mixed up. There's nipples on the coffee table and diapers in the kitchen and formula in the dining room and papers everywhere and chinese food and beer bottles—what is this, batteries, I'm sitting on the batteries.

DAVID: Just what I need.

SUSAN: What I need is some organization.

DAVID: It's been a little hectic, Suze. We just had a baby, we are allowed to be a little disorganized.

SUSAN: It's hurting my head.

DAVID: Look let's get through tonight and I will organize everything okay. Just hold your baby. And—be happy. That's all you have to do. (*Beat*) You don't look happy.

(*Pause*)

SUSAN: I hate the smell of these flowers. It's like a funeral home in here.

DAVID: As soon as I'm done here, I will throw them out.

SUSAN: I don't know why people send flowers to begin with.

DAVID: Because they care about you.

(SUSAN suddenly bursts into tears, sobbing)

DAVID: What did I say? What's the matter? People caring, does that upset you?

SUSAN: That's not why.

DAVID: Talk to me. I can't read your mind.

SUSAN: I'm terrified, David. I have never in my life been so terrified. How am I going to keep her alive?

DAVID: Of course you'll keep her—

SUSAN: *How?* I don't know *how.* I'm afraid I'm going to make mistakes.

DAVID: Of course we'll make mistakes. "Parenting is not an exact science." I read that somewhere.

SUSAN: That's cooking. This is a human being.

DAVID: Yes, a human being who wants to stay alive. She's got instincts that will make sure she gets what she needs.

SUSAN: But I don't know what she needs.

DAVID: She'll tell you. That's why she cries. Remember, that's how she communicates. They told us that in the pre-parenting class.

SUSAN: They told us nothing in that class! Nothing! They left out the most important thing. Like how to open up your heart and let something so fragile, so vulnerable, so fucking needy in.

DAVID: Oh. *(Something else he's read)* Bonding doesn't happen automatically for some women-

SUSAN: Oh God that's not it, David, that's not it. *(Pause)* I don't think I can take care of her. Not-not the way I am.

DAVID: You just had a baby. You're exhausted. You need some sleep. We'll take shifts. You go to sleep first and I'll stay up if she cries—

SUSAN: No, no, no, I couldn't sleep. I'm never going to sleep again.

DAVID: Look, she's asleep.

(He takes baby from SUSAN who holds on for a moment, before he gently lays baby down.)

DAVID: Let's put her in her bassinet.

(He winds up a lullaby toy. They stare at the baby.)

SUSAN: She is beautiful.

DAVID: Yes, she is, and so are you.

SUSAN: You must be delirious.

DAVID: Deliriously happy. Sit down, here, lean on me.

(He pulls her down next to him on loveseat)

SUSAN: What about the monitor?

DAVID: *(Snaps in batteries, turns it on)* Done. One by the bassinet. One for our room. And one you can carry around. Okay? The other one can go upstairs. You're all set.

(DAVID hands SUSAN the monitor who holds onto it like a life line, a red light glows, and a low sound of static)

DAVID: Be happy, Susan, for once, just let yourself be happy.

SUSAN: Okay. *(Pause)* I keep feeling like I should be doing something. That I've left something unfinished.

DAVID: The work is done, she's here, she's perfect. We're a family now. We'll get used to it. You will.

SUSAN: *(Tries to smile)* Whatever you say.

DAVID: Now close your eyes. You don't have to sleep, just keep your eyes closed.

(SUSAN closes her eyes. When DAVID is sure her eyes are closed, he closes his. But as the lights begin to fade, SUSAN's eyes slowly open. The red light on the monitor she holds continues to glow. A static white noise sound grows in the darkness. Right before the lights fade out, the ten year old girl appears on stage. SUSAN and she stare at each other silently.)

Scene Four

(Lights rise again in the middle of the night. The baby is howling. SUSAN is frantically rocking her and trying to mix a bottle of formula. Suddenly the baby is quiet. Under the wind outside in the snowstorm, the sound of chimes has abruptly quieted the baby.)

SUSAN: Do you hear that? Do you hear the chimes outside? Yes. Yes. Pretty sound. Pretty. Thank you God.

(She sits down, baby starts fussing again; she gets up immediately and walks back to where they can hear the chimes)

SUSAN: Make a list. Buy chimes. For every room in the house. *(Beat)* Why don't you stop staring at me from the corner and come out here? I know you're there.

GIRL: *(She emerges)* I didn't think you wanted me. Now that you have *her*.

SUSAN: Oh come on. You're here aren't you? If I didn't want you, you wouldn't be here.

GIRL: I can go sleep in the garage. You'd probably like that.

SUSAN: Oh please stop. I can't take criticism right now.

GIRL: You made a promise. Remember?

SUSAN: I don't remember anything beyond the last five minutes and even that is vague.

GIRL: Can I sit by you?

SUSAN: When I sit.

GIRL: I miss you.

SUSAN: I miss me too. Okay...commere.

(*The* GIRL *walks to her and leans up against her, looking at the baby.*)

SUSAN: Hey, can you try mixing that bottle? Two scoops. I think. Wait a minute. No. This is four ounces so four, no, right two two scoops, one, two. I can still count, that's something. Shake it, thank you.

(GIRL *does so, hands her bottle, woman feeds baby*)

GIRL: She's cute.

SUSAN: Mmm.

GIRL: I like her when she's quiet.

(*They feed the baby in silence*)

GIRL: LOOK! She's asleep. YAY!!

SUSAN: Shhh! Don't wake her. (*As she puts baby back in bassinet, suddenly verbablizing her fear*) I think I'm a bad mother.

GIRL: You're not. You just need to get used to it. (*Hands her baby book*) Here, write in your diary. It will make you feel better. Writing in my diary always makes me feel better. Remember?

SUSAN: (*Takes book, searches for pen*) This house is a battlefield.

GIRL: *(Finds pen)* Here! Found one. See, everything's going to be all right.

(SUSAN sits on couch near bassinet, GIRL snuggles next to her)

GIRL: What are we going to write?

SUSAN: *(Writing)* I think I am...

GIRL: A GOOD MOTHER.

SUSAN: *(Still trying to write)* I *want* to be a good mother. Good, good, good. Good mother. But I can't think straight. *(Struggling to find the words)* My thoughts... dissolve...like sugar...in water. Ow. Don't lean on me like that.

GIRL: What's wrong with your boobs, they're like rocks.

SUSAN: I'm being *punished* for not *breastfeeding.*

GIRL: Write about the baby.

SUSAN: She is so tiny, and yet so *huge* there is not enough room in this house for her. She takes up every available space, fills every corner. She is a *whale* that swam, no, an *ocean liner* that has parked itself right inside the middle of my life.

GIRL: But isn't she cute?

SUSAN: She is. She's cute. She's heartbreakingly beautiful. But her sweet little round head worries me. The soft spots. I try not to touch them, but I watch my fingers being drawn there, tracing, the delicate membrane if anybody pushed—

GIRL: DON'T—!

(GIRL takes book away)

GIRL: My turn. "Baby's First Day Home:" The day I have waited for all my life has finally arrived. My beautiful adorable incredibly cute little baby is here. I

am holding her right now and letting her know how
much I love her every single second since she is alive
so that she never has to wonder if it's true.

SUSAN: I do love her. I just have this funny feeling. Like
doom. Like something bad is going to happen.

GIRL: Nothing bad will happen as long as you take care
of your baby. And love her. Keep loving her. *Always.*

*(Husband enters. He has a gigantic baby's head for a head.
SUSAN stares. GIRL doesn't seem to notice anything wrong,
but senses SUSAN's fear.)*

DAVID: What are you doing? It's three A M. Come to
bed.

SUSAN: She's in the bassinet.

DAVID: So put her in the crib.

SUSAN: But she might wake up.

DAVID: I'll do it.

SUSAN: NO! Don't touch her!

DAVID: Suze, what's the matter?

SUSAN: You're scaring me.

DAVID: She's my daughter; I'm not going to hurt her.
You gotta let me help. *(Gently picks up baby)* See. Out
like a light. I'll put her upstairs. And then I'll come and
get you. If you can't sleep I'll just hold you. *(He carries
baby upstairs, exits)*

SUSAN: Not with that head you won't.

*(SUSAN stays huddled on the couch. DAVID re-enters with
his normal head. Pulls SUSAN up from couch)*

DAVID: Come on, baby, let me put you to bed. You're
exhausted.

(He leads her to bed. GIRL *stays seated, reaching out to turn the volume up on baby monitor so she can hear them going upstairs, getting into bed, soft talking from* DAVID, *then baby sounds: grunts, breath etc, come from monitor. Then:* DAVID's *sleeping breath.* SUSAN *softly weeping)*

*(*MARCÉ *has entered and stands talking to the* GIRL *who listens intently)*

MARCÉ: We cannot ignore the brief episodes of tears and sadness, lability of mood, with mild confusion, experienced by all if not most new mother's. We call this "milk fever" as it begins on the third day after delivery when the milk flow begins and ends by the tenth day. However, the mental alienation we observe in women who have just given birth offers infinite variety in how it manifests and in prognosis, making it difficult to draw general conclusions. *(He sits opposite* GIRL *and continues.)* Sometimes in the first days, it begins with a few isolated ideas of a sad nature. These wrong conceptions appear benign at first, but in fact are very dangerous. Sometimes we observe a global excitation that is closer to mania, and only later those symptoms change to depression. Not the least curious however are the auditory and visual hallucinations that can occur when the patient wakes or is going to sleep. These hallucinations are not considered mental alienation because the women are aware of their state, they know they are going through a morbid phenomena. *(Standing)* But if the state goes on and they are harassed by voices following them day and night, the patient becomes agitated and worried. Their spirit and mind becomes influenced by these hallucinations, and then it is easy to understand how an incoherent and fearless action can be taken. *(Exiting)* The most frequent outcome, with time, is recovery. Long baths can be useful, but the most recommended treatment is surveillance.

(He exits. The GIRL *remains holding monitor. Fade to black)*

Scene Five

(Daytime. SUSAN *sits at the table filling out forms. She sits stiffly, her breasts painfully engorged. Baby monitor sits on table next to her, spewing static. Every once in a while the baby grunts or moans and* SUSAN *strains to listen, until she returns to her forms)*

SUSAN: How would you describe your stay at the hospital? Satisfactory? Unsatisfactory. *(Writing)* Hell.

(Baby makes noise on monitor. SUSAN *freezes)*

SUSAN: How would you describe your support system: extended family, mother or mother in law, sisters, friends, husband, no support system. Circle all that apply... *(Writing)* Husband...No support system. *(Beat)* How would you describe your mood: Happy, sad, confused. Choose one. *(Stuck)* Confused. *(She brings monitor close to her ear, shakes it.)* How often have you cried since you brought your baby home: Once, twice, three times, every day. *(Writing)* Every five minutes. *(Tearing, fighting it)* How would you describe the way you care for your baby? Confident, hesitant, someone else takes care of the baby. *(Pause, then writing)* Other. *(Reading)* How would you describe your overall experience of motherhood? *(Laughs outloud)* Hahaha! *(Writing)* Like being hit by a train. *(Reading)* Have you had thoughts of hurting yourself or your baby? Have you had obsessive thoughts about hurting the baby that frighten you? That you don't seem able to control? Have you hurt your baby? *(Writing)* No!

*(*DAVID *suddenly enters with bag from drugstore)*

SUSAN: *Yes!* Oh, David, it was horrible, I nearly loped off the top of her finger, there was blood pouring I couldn't believe how much blood from her tiny finger—

DAVID: *(Overlapping)* What bleeding? What are you talking about? Did you take her to the hospital? Did you call the doctor? Where is she, is she alright?

SUSAN: No, no, yes, she's all right now.

DAVID: Just tell me what happened.

SUSAN: I was cutting her fingernails and I cut her finger instead, the top of her tiny little finger, it started bleeding and she started screaming, it took me an hour to calm her down.

DAVID: Is she sleeping now?

SUSAN: She's sleeping now and so I came down here and thought I would sit at the table like a human being and fill out these forms from the hospital so I would feel like I got something done but instead, they are making me feel like a whacko—

DAVID: You're not a whacko—

SUSAN: *(Waving the paper at him)* But I cry every day, I cry everyday several times a day, every time the baby cries I cry, when she finally stops crying, I cry from relief, at night I am so tired, I cry, and in the morning I cry because I can't believe it's morning already.

DAVID: I wish I could cry.

SUSAN: But don't you think that's a lot of crying?

DAVID: I do. But I also think there's been a huge change in your life. You're dealing with a lot. And you're worried because I'm going back to work tomorrow, I know you are.

SUSAN: I don't want to think about that now.

DAVID: Forget the forms. Put them down. I got the ace bandage. How are your breasts?

(SUSAN *stands up and painfully unzips her shirt and takes it off facing* DAVID *upstage, who cringes when he sees them.)*

DAVID: Are you sure about this?

SUSAN: My mother said to bind them with an ace bandage.

(As he does, she winces in pain as he tries to get the bandages straight.)

SUSAN: She also said to drink epson salts.

DAVID: You're not going to do that.

SUSAN: It's slipping David, please just put it on, wrap it around, the more you stimulate them the worse it's going to get.

DAVID: I'm sorry, Susan. Your mother should be here.

SUSAN: My mother has her own life and that's fine. If she were here she'd be driving me crazy. I can go crazy on my own.

DAVID: Want me to call my mother, see if she'll come now?

SUSAN: No, God, no.

DAVID: *(Trying humor)* My wife the porn star.

SUSAN: *(Crying)* I used to be a powerful woman, I had a job, I made decisions everyday, I hired and fired people. I used to make other people cry.

DAVID: You're crying because you're in pain. *(As he wraps)* Is this normal, have you talked to the doctor about it?

SUSAN: He said wear a tight fitting bra, I tried to tell him that my tits are two rock hard eggplants that no bra invented is going to fit, tight or otherwise, but all he said was no stimulation and it should be over in a few days.

DAVID: How's that?

SUSAN: That's good. (*Acknowledging his effort*) Thank you, David. I know it hasn't been easy for you either.

DAVID: I'm sorry you have to go through all this.

SUSAN: David. Sometimes I have these ideas that come into my head. They just pop into my head, I'm not thinking about it, or planning anything, I'll just suddenly have this idea out of the blue. This...thought.

DAVID: What kind of thought?

SUSAN: Thoughts, actually.

DAVID: What kind of thoughts?

(*She struggles to explain, the baby starts crying on the monitor.* GIRL *appears*)

SUSAN: Oh, there's the baby.

DAVID: I'll get her. You sit.

(SUSAN *sits at table,* DAVID *goes upstairs. We hear him cooing and talking to baby.* SUSAN *listens.* GIRL *approaches her from behind*)

DAVID: Hey little princess, where's Daddy's little girl. Don't cry, shhhh, that's a girl...shhhh. There, there, Daddy's got you now. Safe and sound.

(*The* GIRL *puts her hand on* SUSAN's *shoulder, who acknowledges her silently*)

GIRL: I'm keeping the promise I made. (*Sits at the table across from* SUSAN) Remember, when Mommy got D-R-U-N-K, and slapped me in the face because I had a fight with the babysitter. She was mad because she called the bar and told her to come home. It wasn't the first time she slapped me, and it wasn't the last time either. It was the worst time because I was expecting comfort and got the opposite. Later when I sat on the edge of my bed in the dark, rocking myself to calm down, I made a promise to her then. I promised I would never hit my child. No matter what. If I ever had one, I would take care of her always, and never ever let her think I didn't love her.

SUSAN: *(Trying to ignore her, returning to forms)* Have you heard or seen things that no one else does?

(SUSAN gathers the forms and tears them up)

Scene Six

(The baby is screaming, SUSAN is trying to change baby's diaper. GIRL sits nearby her nose in a science textbook, reading and taking notes. Four small paper cups filled with dirt are lined up in front of her. A bag of unshelled peanuts is opened on the table. The girl shells and eats the peanuts as she reads, occasionally aloud To SUSAN who wrestles with baby, trying to change its diaper. MARCÉ sits in the corner observing, taking notes.)

SUSAN: I've been afraid to say it but I think she has colic.

GIRL: *(Nose in book)* What's colic?

SUSAN: Unexplained crying.

GIRL: All babies have colic.

SUSAN: If you eat all those peanuts you'll get a stomach ache.

GIRL: *(Counting peanuts)* One in the dark, no water. One in the dark, with water. One in the light, no water. One in the light with water.

SUSAN: You would think I was killing her.

GIRL: She's probably cold. *(Reading from her book)*
All plants and animals need energy to live. Energy
comes from food and oxygen. Or she's hungry.
Animals eat plants or other animals that eat plants,
so all food comes from plants. Animals breathe in
oxygen and breathe out carbon dioxide. Or she pooped.
Plants use carbon dioxide to make food and oxygen.
Life on earth depends on plants.

SUSAN: Can you shut off that monitor that sound drives
me crazy.

GIRL: *(Continues reading)* Reproduction takes place in
the flower where ouvles become seeds. The seed takes
food from the plant and begins to grow into an embryo.
Water seeps into the seed which begins to swell. Once
a seed absorbs enough water, the embryo grows into a
baby plant.

SUSAN: *(Finally gets baby dressed, quiet, after a pause)*
I don't know what to do with her.

GIRL: *(Puts book down)* Play with her. Hey baby, can
you smile for me? There you go, there's a pretty smile.
Unwrap her, you have her wrapped up too tight.
She can't move like that. There you go. This little piggy
went to the market...she likes it...this little piggy stayed
home...this little piggy had roast beef and this little
piggy...

SUSAN: Had none...but this little piggy cried wee wee
wee all the way home.

GIRL: Do it again.

SUSAN: She has my toes. Look at that. Those are my
toes; the second one is longer than the first. That's a
sign of intelligence. My mother told me.

GIRL: I thought it meant you'd be bossy. Here...little
boss, tickle, tickle, tickle. She's smiling.

SUSAN: Probably gas.

GIRL: That's a smile. I know a smile when I see a smile. Yes, yes. Smile for your mommy, little peanut.

SUSAN: *(Laughing)* You know how to play with her. *(Pause)* What's wrong with me I don't even know how to play with my own baby?

GIRL: *(Singing)* Found a peanut, found a peanut, found a peanut last night, last night I found a peanut, found a peanut last night....

(Monitor crackles with static)

GIRL *(Cont'd)* It was rotten, it was rotten, it was rotten last night, last night it was rotten——

SUSAN: I asked you to shut that monitor off.

MONITOR: *(SUSAN's voice echoes)* Don't know how to play with your own baby.

GIRL: Ate it anyway, ate it anyway——

SUSAN: Shut it off!

GIRL: Sorry.

(SUSAN throw monitor across the room knocking over the GIRL'S peanuts and cups. GIRL starts picking up the peanuts and putting them back in their cups. MARCÉ helps GIRL with her experiment.)

(The baby starts fussing again, SUSAN picks her up just a little too roughly, and starts bouncing/rocking her.)

GIRL: Plant one in the dark, no water. One in the dark, water. One in the light, no water. One in the light, water.

(As the baby's fussing increases, SUSAN becomes more and more agitated, MARCÉ observes this)

SUSAN: What?! What is wrong?! I'm going to throw you out the goddamn window if you don't shut up! Something is wrong with her.

GIRL: Take her to the doctor if you think something is wrong.

SUSAN: *(Baby in one arm, violently packing diaper bag)* Fine, we're going now, we're going right now.

Scene Seven

(DOCTOR's office. The pediatrician from the hospital is examining the baby. MARCÉ has followed SUSAN into this scene and sits on one side of DOCTOR with notes, SUSAN holds her questions to ask on a torn piece of paper)

DOCTOR: Have you given this baby a bath? Look under here. *(She cleans under baby's chin.)* You've got to wash under the folds, especially under the chin. We could grow potatoes under here! *(Voiceover) Or peanuts!* *(Normal)* Don't feel bad. *(Voiceover, echoes) Bad. Mother.* *(Normal)* Everyone forgets. Just make sure you do it from now on. *(Voiceover) Asshole.*

SUSAN: I'm—sorry. I—will.

DOCTOR: How is everything else going? Are you adjusting to motherhood all right? Are you getting any sleep? Hahahaha.

SUSAN: Not much. I think I'm having trouble adjusting.

DOCTOR: That's normal.

SUSAN: I used to be a competent person...now I feel...incompetent.

DOCTOR: That's normal.

SUSAN: I feel like I don't know the right thing to do. When to pick her up, when to put her down.

DOCTOR: It's all right with me if you never put her down.

SUSAN: When to feed her, when to do something else.

DOCTOR: Feed on demand.

SUSAN: I feel like I don't have the right *food* to keep her *alive.*

(The echoey sound continues to bother SUSAN*)*

DOCTOR: You're— *(Voice over) Strange. (Normal)* You're formula feeding.

SUSAN: Yes. And I...well I guess I'm afraid of the formula. What is it but chemicals really—

DOCTOR: Essentially everything is chemical.

SUSAN: —and I worry about things like, what if I run out, or if the world suddenly ran out—

DOCTOR: That's ridiculous. *(Voiceover) Idiot.*

SUSAN: And, you know: tampering. Which I try not to think about.

DOCTOR: Tampering?

SUSAN: By terrorists.

*(*SUSAN *laughs to cover her extreme fear.* DOCTOR *laughs with her.)*

DOCTOR: *(Brief pause)* You chose not to breastfeed and I know you had your reasons, but if you've had a change of heart and were really committed it may not be too late with continuous sucking to stimulate some mild lactation.

SUSAN: That would be...too much to bear.

DOCTOR: I thought that's what you wanted.

SUSAN: That's not what I'm saying.

DOCTOR: What are you saying?

SUSAN: Do you think I should worry?

DOCTOR: About what.

SUSAN: About...terrorists.

DOCTOR: What about terrorists?

SUSAN: Tampering with the formula. Or kidnapping. Or biological weapons. Or blowing us up if I take her outside...

DOCTOR: No.

(But she writes that down)

DOCTOR: Anything else?

SUSAN: Sometimes...I have...these...funny ideas. Hahahaha.

DOCTOR: "Funny", like the terrorists?

SUSAN: No. These are like. Oh, you know...like the baby is crying and crying and crying, and I think oops...dropped her. Hahaha. Or what would happen if I just...

DOCTOR: Threw her out the window. Right, right, well you're not gonna do that, right?

SUSAN: Right, right.

DOCTOR: Then it's normal.

SUSAN: Normal.

DOCTOR: Part of what we call *crazy normal*. Because becoming a mother is so *insane*. But it's within the range of normal just so long as know it's *crazy* but you don't *act* on it. Have you tried keeping a journal? Putting these "thoughts" down on paper. Might help you put things into perspective.

SUSAN: My mother gave me a journal—

DOCTOR: Good, good, good.

SUSAN: But what I wrote disturbed me.

DOCTOR: That's fine. We can't always be *happy happy happy* all the time. Right? How "normal" would that be? Motherhood is a lot of *work*. You don't sleep, you don't have time to eat or shower or go to the movies or do any of the things you used to do for yourself. You're going to have some negative feelings. Okay. So...did you want to switch to the soy?

SUSAN: You have to wonder how the human race has continued for so long. If this is motherhood. *(Beat)* She's already on the soy.

DOCTOR: Oh. *(Beat)* Then why don't we stick with it?

(SUSAN *and* MARCÉ *wait as the* DOCTOR *makes her notes.* MARCÉ *observes* SUSAN *a moment longer.)*

DOCTOR: Don't forget the bath. For baby. And you too if you want. I find long baths very relaxing. Don't be afraid to pamper yourself.

(Fade to next scene)

Scene Eight

(The sound of water rushing into a tub. A baby bathtub is on the floor. SUSAN *kneels over it, with soap, wash cloths, etc.* GIRL *is nearby holding a rubber duck. Woman leans baby back into bath.)*

SUSAN: There we go, there, there, don't be afraid. It's just water. I won't let you go, I gotcha. I gotcha. *(She uses wash cloth as a sponge, squeezing water over the baby)* I think she likes it. She looks like she likes it. She's not screaming.

GIRL: *(Splashing as she puts rubber duck into baby's face)* See the rubber ducky! *Quack! Quack!*—

SUSAN: Easy!

GIRL: *(Pulling back)* Sorry.

SUSAN: I know you want to play. I'm just nervous.
Go ahead, play.

GIRL: *(Places rubber duck in bath)* It's okay.

SUSAN: You want to try? *(Holds out washcloth)*

GIRL: *(Brightening up immediately)* Yeah! *(Takes wash cloth and repeats what SUSAN was doing; singing)* This is the way we take a bath, take a bath, take a bath, this is the way we take a bath, take a bath, take a bath...

(SUSAN and the GIRL laugh together at the baby's reaction in the bath.

SUSAN: *(Relaxes a moment, letting GIRL wash baby, listening to her sing and hum as she recounts her dream)* I had this weird dream. I dreamt I was taking clothes out of the washer, and there was something dark and sopping wet at the bottom of the washer, jeans or something, and I had to yank to get them out, and when I did, it was the baby. Actually two babies and I had to decide which one was the real baby. They looked exactly the same, but I knew I had to choose one so I did, and dropped one in the garbage can, which landed with a thud and didn't move, so I figured I had chosen the right one. But the baby I kept lay on the changing table with her eyes closed not moving, so I worried I picked the wrong one. The changing table changed into a large piece of white paper. There was a knife lying on the paper. I knew I had to cut her open and find her tiny organs, to discover how they worked. I had to dissect her in order to know if it was the right baby, so I could take care of her. She was splayed on the paper like a little frog and I watched my arm reach for the knife, saw my hand pick it up and push the knife in, like a surgeon. I heard a little pop and then it slid right in, but I couldn't find any organs, just blood, blood in the bathtub, and I couldn't find the baby because she was under the water; all I could see were my own hands holding her under the water. *(Brief pause)* It would be so easy to push her head under the water.

GIRL: *(Picking baby up, wrapping her in a towel)* Bathtime's over. I gotcha. There, there. I gotcha.

(GIRL crosses with baby in towel. SUSAN sits staring at water in tub. GIRL rocks baby on other side of the room, throwing one backward glance at SUSAN still kneeling in front of tub.)

(Cross fade to next scene)

Scene Nine

(DAVID and SUSAN are sitting cross-legged on the floor eating chinese food from cartons, drinking beer from two bottles. The baby is asleep upstairs. The monitor is on, low. The GIRL is sitting on the stairs a shadow listening.)

SUSAN: *(Laughing, relaxed)* So...what do you think... should we put her up for adoption?

DAVID: *(Laughing also)* Yeah, right...you're kidding right?

SUSAN: *(Still laughing, then)* No. Actually. *(Beat)* Okay, half kidding. Sense of humor *check!*

DAVID: Hahaha. The answer is still no. Want your fortune, Mommy Dearest? *(Takes two fortune cookies, holds them out to her)* Pick.

SUSAN: I want a wise one, not a stupid one. Please give me some wisdom. *(Cracks open cookie reads)* Patience is the key to joy. Well, I got the stupid one.

DAVID: *(Reading)* Take advantage of sleeping baby and make love to your wife.

SUSAN: Okay, you got the stupid one.

DAVID: *(Opening a third cookie)* There is no such thing as stupid fortune cookie. *(Embracing her)* Your breasts are better. I'll be gentle.

(She stiffens, then pulls a little away from him. Rebuffed, he is hurt.)

SUSAN: Please, David. I've had this baby attached to me all day long the last thing I want is someone touching my body.

DAVID: I'm sorry I have desire for my wife.

SUSAN: It's not...personal.

DAVID: Oh no, my wife doesn't want me to touch her or go near her or show any kind of affection.

SUSAN: *(Trying to explain)* It's not that, David it's—
Look, you go to work. You get out of this house.
You have the outside world stimulating you. I am stuck here hour after hour after hour the physical source of everything for this little vacuum cleaner that leaves me completely empty by the end of the day. I'm sorry most of the time there's nothing left over.

DAVID: I thought having a baby was going to "fulfill you".

SUSAN: It did. Okay, it did. Now I'm drowning in fulfillment.

DAVID: You confuse the hell out of me.

SUSAN: Look, I had a job, I did things, I made decisions, I took phone calls, I went out to lunch, I had a date book where I wrote down my schedule, I worked late, worked weekends—

DAVID: And you hated it. You wanted to quit. You wanted a baby you said, you needed a baby to make your life complete. You said—

SUSAN: I said I was burnt out, I wanted some time off. A Caribbean vacation would've done it.

DAVID: I would've taken you to the Bahamas, but I heard "Baby."

SUSAN: Yes, a baby, a happy, smiling, loving, responsive child who loved me back.

DAVID: She loves you.

SUSAN: She's a loaf of bread, she doesn't know love, she only knows if she's dry or full or warm.

DAVID: That's not true, she's going to grow out of this stage, she's going to learn to walk and talk and—

SUSAN: I know that—but the way it feels, it is so far into the future that it's inconceivable to me—

DAVID: Maybe you need to get out more. Go to lunch with your girl friends.

SUSAN: Ha! Girlfriends? I don't have any girlfriends anymore.

DAVID: Yes you do.

SUSAN: Where are they? Terri visited me *once* in the hospital. And nobody else has come, because they're not interested in babies.

DAVID: You have to pick up the phone, Susan. They probably think you're busy.

SUSAN: They're the ones who are too busy.

DAVID: Well then you've got to meet other mothers, who are going through the same thing you are. But in order to meet them, you've got to go out, go to the park.

SUSAN: It's freezing, everything is covered in ice.

DAVID: Go to the museum, a coffee shop—go to the grocery store.

SUSAN: I'd rather kill myself.

DAVID: I don't know what to tell you.

(Pause)

SUSAN: *(Tries again)* I know it sounds like I'm
complaining, believe me, I hear it in my head all
day long, but I don't know how else to say it. How
unprepared I feel, how lonely, how happy other
mothers are; how humiliating to admit to anyone,
to you, even to myself that I am not—happy.

DAVID: I'm sure other first time mothers feel like that.

SUSAN: Are they afraid all the time, like I am?

DAVID: What is there to be afraid of? If you got out of
this house—

SUSAN: *(Trying again to explain)* But see, I'm afraid to
take her out, it's too much, bringing the formula and
diapers and getting her in and out of her suit and then
the car seat and god what if she has a melt down in
public, I don't think I can handle it. I'd get anxious and
sweaty and I'd fall apart in the middle of the street.

DAVID: Look, Susan. I know it's hard. But I know you.
And I know you can handle it. You just have to figure
out how. Be methodical about it. Make a list, check it
off. You've got to try. I can't always be here to help you.
I've got to work. And— *(Pause)* And I've got to go on a
trip. For work.

(Beat)

SUSAN: When were you going to tell me?!

DAVID: I'm telling you now. I've got to go to Chicago;
it's only ten days, to check on the blah blah blah blah
blahbity blah—

(He becomes incoherent as static on monitor grows.)

SUSAN: You can't. Tell them you can't. No, David,
I can't be alone with this baby. What can I say to make
you understand? Listen, please listen to me. I've been
having thoughts.

DAVID: What are you talking about?

SUSAN: Unbidden thoughts. And dreams and voices
sort of. Not, not like I'm hearing voices, I'm not that far
gone yet, I don't think, more like words in my head.

DAVID: What are the words saying?

SUSAN: I'm afraid to say it out loud to you, you might
think I might really do something. Like when I'm
exhausted and the baby's been fussin all day and I
suddenly think: what if I found something hard, like
the molding in the doorway and I just bash her head
against it. Or, what if I bite off all her fingers. Her
fingers are so soft, like steamed stringbeans. It would be
so easy to—but of course I would never do those things.
Hurt my tiny soft vulnerable screaming red package of
love. (Beat) I hate this.

DAVID: Hate what?

SUSAN: I don't know how to be a mother.

DAVID: So you'll learn.

SUSAN: But I don't want to be the mother!

DAVID: What are you talking about, you are the mother.
I can't be the mother, I'm the father. Who has to go to
work and make money so I can buy things we need,
because the needs keep growing but the leash is getting
shorter and shorter. I can't do both, be here and work;
it's not possible.

SUSAN: Don't misunderstand me. I love her. She has
swallowed my heart and soul and that is what is so
terrifying. I've been sucked down into this terrifyingly
dependent black creature hole and I can't breathe half

the time I actually have to remind myself to breathe
half the time; I think I'm drowning literally under
water, because it's too much pressure. To keep her
alive and make sure she develops the right way and
grows up to be a decent human being who is going to
contribute to society and be well adjusted and *happy*,
no wonder the human race is so *fucked up*. They leave
that to *one person*, while the father, the father goes away
on business trips to Chicago leaving the *crazy mother*
home to take care of this tenuous, fragile, paper thin
life, it's too much responsibility for one person.

DAVID: You're not making any sense. I have to work.

SUSAN: I know you have to work, I know you—you do.
But that's my point. I used to work and so I know about
work, and I know when a person works, they get paid
and they get breaks. I know you get breaks, your drive
on the parkway—

DAVID: You gotta be kiddin me—

SUSAN: —*is a twenty minute break*. If you go on this
trip to Chicago, I won't get any breaks! It will be one
continuous loop for twenty-four hours times seven
days a week! I'd rather be a janitor in a nuclear
waste dump then spend the rest of my life doing
this twenty-four/seven!

DAVID: You're telling me you would rather shovel
radioactive shit, instead of caring for your beautiful
newborn baby girl on your own for one week.

SUSAN: You said ten days, and I'm saying, I don't think
I should be left alone, just me and her, for too long and
a week or whatever it is, is *too long.*

DAVID: The last thing I want to do is go on this trip,
but I've already bailed out on two others, I didn't even
tell you about. I can't be regional manager without
going to the regional offices.

SUSAN: *(After a long pause, much quieter)* Please don't leave me alone, David. Please.

DAVID: You're letting your fear overtake you. It won't be that bad.

SUSAN: For you, it won't be bad for you. You'll be drinking martinis in your hotel room, relaxing in front of the T V—

DAVID: You're making this harder for both of us.

SUSAN: Forget about me, to hell with me. Think about her. Your defenseless daughter lying in her crib. Would you leave her alone for ten days with a mentally ill nanny? No, no you wouldn't leave her alone for ten minutes.

DAVID: You are not mentally ill. Stop talking yourself into this. I've been more than patient, Susan, I've been supportive and understanding and have done far more than most husbands and what have I gotten for it? I've had no acknowledgement, no affection, no physical response from you. I've got no one to listen to me about my hard day, or my problems at work or my fears or difficulties being a father. You're not the only one having an adjustment. But that doesn't get acknowledged. Just the opposite, heap on the guilt the blame and no matter how hard I try to make things better or easier for you it's never enough.

SUSAN: If you love me you won't go.

DAVID: I'm going because I love you. Because I love my family and I want to provide a good home for them. That's my life now. And Susan, this is your life. The sooner you accept that the happier we'll all be.

SUSAN: I can't. I don't. I'm not.

DAVID: It will end. The week will come to an end.

SUSAN: *(Exploding)* You said *ten days*!

(Sound from monitor as it begins to crackle. She gets up, frantic, paces the room once and then picks up the baby's bouncey seat, smashing it several times, before tossing it to him, as if to say: see?)

DAVID: You scare me.

SUSAN: My point exactly.

MONITOR: *(A clear woman's voice:)* Bad mother.

SUSAN: What? Did you hear...?

DAVID: I didn't hear anything. *(He exits.)*

GIRL: *(Sadly from her perch where she's been listening to the entire scene)* It said you are a bad mother.

SUSAN: Do you believe it?

GIRL: Do you?

(SUSAN and GIRL look fearfully at each other. Baby starts fussing)

Scene Ten

(The baby is sleeping. GRANDMA sits in rocking chair, rocking baby silently behind SUSAN who squats on the floor, rocking herself back and forth, staring straight ahead, almost catatonic. The GIRL is curled up across from SUSAN filling out the baby diary. MARCÉ is also there, taking notes.)

GIRL: This journal belongs to... *(Writes)* And was recorded by... *(Writes)* Baby was born on... At... She weighed... And was...inches long. Okay. *(Asks SUSAN)* What were your first words when you saw your new baby for the first time?

SUSAN: *(Thinking for a second)* ..."Is it out yet?"

(GIRL stops writing)

GIRL: She is going to read this when she gets older. You should at least make an effort. *(Beat)* Baby's Routine.

SUSAN: Baby wakes up. Crying. Mommy makes bottle. Feeds baby bottle. Baby sometimes drinks bottle, burps, pukes, poops. Screams as diaper is changed. Resists sleep at all costs. Red faced screaming gasping finally out of exhaustion falls into sleep. Mommy stares into darkness all night long, standing guard until baby wakes up. Crying.

GIRL: Okay then, a typical day in Mommy's life now:

SUSAN: I just said. Crying. Staring into darkness long into the night, standing guard, waiting for baby who wakes up crying. Makes bottle, feeds baby, changes baby, begs baby to stop crying, cries, that's Mommy crying now, because Mommy needs sleep, and although sleep doesn't come anymore, she dreams of sleep with her eyes wide open, a big sleep, in canopy beds and fluffy white pillows, billowing comforters, sinking into black oblivion. If only.

GIRL: Okay. Give me a *happy* baby moment. Go:

(Long pause. After several false starts, SUSAN dictates as GIRL scribbles into book.)

SUSAN: The warmth of your body when you let me hold you. When you are still and let me hold you. Your sleeping breath soft and light and I am rocking you, my arms wrapped around the whole of you. It feels, then, like someone is holding me too and for a moment, I am being rocked and breathing my own quiet sleep. And in that boundless moment, I forget where you end and I begin; in that blank space my thoughts are finally still, and I realize this is all I want.

GIRL: This one's good: if you could tell her one thing you want her to remember as she is growing up, what would it be?

(The ghosts all perk up, lean in to hear SUSAN's *answer.* SUSAN *walks to* GRANDMA, *takes baby from her during the following.)*

SUSAN: Even though I don't know what I am doing. Even though I feel imprisoned and paralyzed. Even though there is a snake in my belly eating my fearful heart for breakfast each morning. I do love you, little heart. And I hope someday you will love me too.

GIRL: *(Happily finishes writing)* Okay.

Scene Eleven

*(*GRANDMA *is gone.* TERRI *is holding the baby, laughing and cooing.* SUSAN *is pouring tea, smiling. The* GIRL *is near* SUSAN. MARCÉ *is also in the room, where* SUSAN *can see him, but out of the way.)*

TERRI: She's such a good baby, Suze. Look how good she is.

SUSAN: Oh yeah, she's always good when other people are around. But the minute you walk out that door...

TERRI: I don't believe it, she's a doll.

SUSAN: She sure is, and she's lucky she's cute, that's all I can say. More tea?

TERRI: No thanks, I'll be up all night.

SUSAN: That's the idea.

TERRI: Is that banana bread, did you bake that? You're incredible.

SUSAN: What is there to mashing up a few bananas?

TERRI: Cut me a piece, it looks good.

SUSAN: The knife is by you.

TERRI: Oh, well, I got my hands full right now. And I don't want to put little miss beautiful down.

SUSAN: You'd be surprised what a person could do with one hand.

TERRI: But I haven't had any practice! Not like you Ms Super Mom already.

SUSAN: Well then no banana bread for Aunt Terri! *(Laughs to cover)* I didn't make it anyway. David picked it up somewhere.

TERRI: I don't care I'm starving. A little piece.

SUSAN: You'll have to give me the baby then. I'm serious, Terri, I don't go near knives anymore. They have some kind of magnetic force that draws your hand right to them, and I don't like the out of control feeling they put out. Bridges do that to me, too. But luckily since I don't go out, Mommy can't jump off one.

TERRI: I think staying home all day with baby is going to your head, Suze.

SUSAN: I'd agree with that.

TERRI: So, when's David leaving, for his trip, you said.

(Baby starts fussing now, gradually, building on and off to the end of scene.)

SUSAN: Sunday afternoon four P M. Can you think of a more dismal time to be abandoned. Hahahaha. I swear if I was ever going to kill myself it would be on a Sunday afternoon at four P M.

TERRI: Let me look at my calendar....I can probably come next week and spell ya. How's Wednesday....

SUSAN: We'll be here.

TERRI: I'll come over after work, if it's not too crazy I can probably get here by six-thirty.

SUSAN: Knives, scissors, nail clippers. I keep all shiny sharp objects out of sight.

TERRI: Are you worried about the baby getting them? She's not even crawling yet.

SUSAN: No, it's not the baby I'm worried about, well, yes, indirectly I am worried about the baby, but it's the knives themselves I'm worried about, Terri, and I've tried telling David, but he won't listen. More tea?

TERRI: I've had enough, thanks.

SUSAN: So have I, but that doesn't stop me. This is like my eighth cup, but it's the only thing that keeps me going.

TERRI: Here let me cut you some bread.

(SUSAN *looks away as* TERRI *picks up knife and cuts a slice of bread.*)

TERRI: We all miss you at work.

SUSAN: Some days there's nothing I want more than to wake up, take a shower, put on a power suit and a pair of pumps and drive to work and stay there for the next sixteen hours.

TERRI: Maybe you should then.

SUSAN: The thought of what that would entail now is too exhausting to entertain. Beginning with the shower.

TERRI: Why don't you go take a shower, I'll watch her.

SUSAN: That's okay.

TERRI: No really, go, go take a shower, you'll feel better.

SUSAN: I'm afraid I won't feel better.

(Pause)

TERRI: Has your Mom been here?

SUSAN: Not until danger of heavy frost is long past.
I won't see her till June or July.

TERRI: Susan, maybe this is a stupid question, and if I'm
out of line, just tell me, but, are you happy?

SUSAN: Of course that's a stupid question.

TERRI: You seem so sad.

SUSAN: No, this is joy, Terri. Maybe since you have
never experienced true joy you don't recognize it.
Mother plus Baby equals Joy.

TERRI: *(Laughing, a little, then)* I can't tell if you're joking
or not.

(Long pause)

SUSAN: Actually, I feel like I'm part of a twisted
science experiment like I'm in a terrarium and someone,
a demented little girl say, is slowly steadily pumping
all of the air out. Just to see what would happen.
Well watch what happens. Take notes.

TERRI: I'm sorry I didn't come sooner. I meant to,
but we've been swamped at work. Which completely
swallowed up all of my time, and then, I know this
doesn't in the least compare, but my cat is like my kid,
and he had another urinary track infection, and the vet
is telling me the next step is like a sex change
operation—

SUSAN: Don't apologize.

TERRI: I've wanted to come, its just I've just been so—

SUSAN: Busy. I know. *(Under her breath)* With your cat.

TERRI: Have you...

SUSAN: Have I what?

TERRI: Have you been to your doctor, since the birth?
Has anyone seen you?

SUSAN: You mean besides the Frenchman?

TERRI: Who?

SUSAN: I've been to the pediatrician.

TERRI: Don't you have to get a check up after?

SUSAN: I am perfectly fine. I can run up and down the stairs, take long baths and fuck my husband, if I wanted to.

TERRI: I know a woman.

SUSAN: No.

TERRI: It can't hurt to talk to somebody about how you're feeling.

SUSAN: Good Bye Terri. Thank You for Coming.

TERRI: There's nothing shameful about needing some help.

SUSAN: Oh I need help, I admit that, but what I don't need is you coming in and out of here flaunting your freedom, wearing your unencumbered life tossed carelessly over your shoulder like a scarf while my life is wrapped so tightly around my throat—

TERRI: My goodness Susan—

SUSAN: Breezing in here and telling me what I need, I need help of course I need help, but why do I need some therapist, some stranger, why don't my friends help me, my sister, my mother, for godsake? Where are all the women in my life now, when I need them?

TERRI: Please Susan, calm down. I want to help you.

SUSAN: Careless. I don't have time for careless people anymore.

TERRI: All right, I'm going. I'm sorry if I upset you. But I think you should talk to somebody. Susan, really you know if this was the other way around that's what you would tell me. Remember when I was depressed after Michael, you told me, Terri get therapy, and I listened to you. You know I'm right.

(The baby is howling by now.)

SUSAN: Okay, okay you're right, I'm crazy, how does that help me?

TERRI: You want me to come back Wednesday?

SUSAN: No.

TERRI: I'm worried about you.

SUSAN: Don't worry about me. Worry about your cat.

TERRI: That's not fair.

SUSAN: Your little visit on Wednesday at six-thirty at night when the day is thankfully blessedly half over is not going to help me, Terri. What I need is someone to be this child's mother. It's a little more involved than cleaning out the cat box and putting food in a dish on the floor. So if you're not prepared for the long haul, just get out of my life, okay, just leave me alone.

(SUSAN turns away from TERRI, and tries to calm the baby who is beyond hysterical now)

SUSAN: Shhhhh. Shhhh. What?

(Ignored, TERRI picks up her coat, and leaves)

SUSAN: Shhh. Shhh. What do you want from me? What??

(SUSAN breaks down, lets out a yelp of rage and kicks over coffee table. Baby screaming)

(Black out)

Scene Twelve

(DOCTOR's *office.* MARCÉ *sits in the corner taking notes as* SUSAN *talks to* DOCTOR.)

DOCTOR: Baby is fine.

SUSAN: Define "fine".

DOCTOR: There is absolutely nothing wrong with her.

SUSAN: So she doesn't have colic?

DOCTOR: I didn't say that. But I didn't say she has it either. We don't believe in colic anymore. At least we don't call it that anymore.

SUSAN: What do you call it now?

DOCTOR: You have a baby that cries a lot.

SUSAN: Oh. That's not very comforting.

DOCTOR: How are you doing?

SUSAN: I cry a lot. Hahahaha. (*Beat, waiting for reaction, then*) In fact that's all I do is cry. I want my husband to stay home and help me, but when he does all I do is yell, my best friend came to visit, finally, and I blew up at her for no reason at all, and yet, at the time, I was so angry. I'm lonely all the time, but then when my husband is around, all he wants to do is have sex and I can't bear the thought of one more person needing something from me. I have these...strange thoughts of weird things, which, you know, we talked about, and which you said was "crazy normal" but I'm afraid that I have moved out of the range of normal into crazy. Hahahaha.

DOCTOR: Would you describe yourself as depressed?

SUSAN: Most of the time I would describe myself as pissed off.

MARCÉ: *(Interjecting to the* DOCTOR*) La patiente a l'impression qu'elle a échoué dans sa tache de mère. [The woman felt like she had failed in her duty as a mother.]*

DOCTOR: I'd say you need to do something for yourself so you don't feel so petty and resentful. Go out and buy yourself a red dress, have your husband take you out to dinner, go to a movie, take a long hot bubble bath.

SUSAN: My husband is going away Sunday on business for ten days.

DOCTOR: I can refer you to a good psychiatrist if that's what you think you need—

SUSAN: Maybe, I don't know.

DOCTOR: But really, as a feminist—and I know you've worked outside the home before baby—but, as a feminist, I've come to think of post-partum depression as a natural response on the part of the woman to the transition to motherhood in a society that doesn't value Stay at Home Mom's. But it's a noble thing you're doing.

SUSAN: It's normal?

DOCTOR: I said noble.

SUSAN: Oh. But what about how I'm feeling? Is that still normal?

MARCÉ: *(Interjects to* DOCTOR*) Il est très important qu'elle ne soit jamais seule avec l'enfant. [It is very important that she is never left alone with the child.]*

DOCTOR: Can someone stay with you and help you out with the baby, while your husband's away. Can't your mother come and visit for a week?

SUSAN: He's going for ten days and no, probably not. I guess I can ask her. *(Starting to cry)*

DOCTOR: I'll get my pad. *(Exits)*

(SUSAN cries, holding baby for comfort. MARCÉ reaches out and touches her hand. SUSAN looks up at him.)

MARCÉ: Madame. When I was a boy we had an old bitch terrier with a wonderful sweet nature, a favorite pet of mine, who was expecting her first litter.

(SUSAN stops crying and listens.)

MARCÉ: I watched with fascination as the little dog's belly swelled and I wondered how she would give birth to the puppies inside her. When it started, I was called out of bed to watch as she pushed each pup out with such force and then tenderly licked each one clean, with all the love and devotion any mother would show. Suddenly without warning, with the birth of the last one, she preceded to bite the heads off each little dog, as if the expulsion of the placenta triggered some murderous impulse.

(SUSAN is still listening, horrified now.)

MARCÉ: With the next litter the bitch delivered, we watched carefully, but as she seemed calm and nurturing towards the puppies, we told ourselves the first cannibalism was a one-time occurrence. Unfortunately when we visited her the following morning, we found the headless puppies lying on the blanket. The heads, we found in various parts of the barn as if she sought to hide the consequences of her actions.

(SUSAN turns away, MARCÉ presses on)

MARCÉ: With the third litter she was allowed to nurse as she seemed normal at the beginning. But as we knew not to trust this seeming mother-love, we removed all but one of the puppies. Snuggled under its mother's belly it was left behind unnoticed. That morning we found its tiny body, waiting for us at the door of the barn. The head was never found.

SUSAN: And the moral of this story is?

MARCÉ: I mean to warn you, *Madame*, I do not believe you are in control.

(She packs up baby and leaves. MARCÉ *sits for a moment, makes another note, then follows her.)*

*(*DOCTOR *returns to empty stage)*

(Fade to black)

Scene Thirteen

*(*SUSAN *is alone, holding the baby and trying to write in her journal)*

SUSAN: Number one: Keep Baby Alive...

*(*MARCÉ *and the* GIRL *are huddled over the earlier peanut experiment.)*

SUSAN: Number two...

MARCÉ: What do you observe?

GIRL: Well, the peanut in the dark, that got no water, did not grow at all. The one that got sunlight, but still no water didn't grow either.

MARCÉ: Go on.

GIRL: The one in the dark that got some water actually did grow, but it was strange, pale and skinny and long like it was reaching out for the light even though it was in a dark box and there wasn't a chance.

MARCÉ: Interesting.

GIRL: Of course the peanut that got both water and light grew into a healthy peanut plant. Green and fat with plenty of leaves.

MARCÉ: And what can you infer from your observations?

GIRL: Obviously plants need both sunlight and water to grow normally. But even in a bad environment they will still try to grow. However, without water nothing will grow. Both Life and Death is determined by water.

(*At the mention of water: sound of running water*)

MARCÉ: Hmm. (*Beat*) You are very bright.

(SUSAN *has not been able to complete the next sentence. She searches, then finds phone. Dials.* MARCÉ *and* GIRL *are quiet through her conversation, at first observing the peanut plants, and then observing her.*)

SUSAN: Mom. It's me. Susan. Your first born. How are you? (*Listens a long time*) Oh, good, the baby's good, listen Mom that's why I'm calling. David's going on a business trip, and it's the first time I'll be alone this long with the baby, and I was wondering if you were still planning on coming to visit if you wanted to come a little sooner, you know the weather is good, it really is, its not bad. Next week. He's going to be gone ten days, so if you could come for even part of it, it would help immensely. (*Beat*) I don't want to be alone with the baby. (*Listens again for a really long time*) Okay...thought I'd see if...no problem...come when you can...she's cute. Yes, she is. A little peanut. (*Brief pause*) Mom, were you ever depressed after your pregnancies?

(SUSAN *stops talking on the phone and speaks directly to* GRANDMA *who is now standing in front of her, listening.*)

SUSAN: I remember you used to stand at the stove frying hamburgers. Dad should've been home by then, but he wasn't and you were pissed off at him, but what

I remember is the look on your face. Closed up like a
fist. I still don't know what I hated worse, the stuffed
silence, the smell of greasy hamburgers, menthol
cigarettes, or the choked feeling of my heart being
clenched in that fist. Maybe that's when I lost it?
My maternal instinct? You think? Maybe that explains
why I haven't a clue about what to do next.

(The baby starts screaming. SUSAN *doesn't move; finally*
GRANDMA *exits. During the following,* SUSAN *will go to
baby and very slowly, mechanically, step by step change
diaper over and over.)*

*(*MARCÉ *addresses* GIRL.*)*

MARCÉ: *(Using peanuts to illustrate)* In my observations
of pregnant, newly delivered and nursing mothers
I was shocked to discover two distinct categories.
Together they present a choreography of neurological
syndromes that don't fall into the normal categories of
depression or psychosis, but leap from one to the other,
forward and back, according to some rhythm I sense,
but cannot name.

GIRL: Really?

MARCÉ: The first starts three days after delivery,
typically of a manic quality including agitation,
insomnia, hallucinations, and confusion. The second
starts six weeks after delivery, including exhaustion,
fatigue, melancholia and a very sad delerium.

GIRL: Go on.

MARCÉ: In both cases the mental illness parallels the
physical changes after childbirth as the woman's organs
move back toward their pre-pregnancy state.

GIRL: Interesting. Can you give me any examples?

MARCÉ: *(Using cups for his examples)* Madame C. A thirty
year old woman, after a normal labor, delivered a

healthy baby. Six days later she was seized by a furious delerium. The first sign was when she put the baby in a stove to cook him. The family stopped her, but only against violent resistance. When I arrived, I required four men to restrain her. She didn't recognize anyone and repeated these words in a strident whisper, "He needs to cook, he's not cooked through." No one could convince her otherwise and when left on her own, she would immediately return to the infant, pick him up and head for the stove. She was treated with ether and immediately fell asleep for several hours. When she awoke she was reasonable, although tired, and, remembered nothing of the incident.

SUSAN: Well, I'm not gonna do that. I'm not gonna bite her head off either.

GIRL: *(Referring to second cup)* And this one.

MARCÉ: Madame V. A woman, thirty-two, after a difficult and very long delivery gave birth to a baby girl. She seemed to recover and although she had difficulty breastfeeding, by the sixth week the baby was nursing, however the mother began to disappear for a few hours every day and sometimes at night was found wandering out by the well staring down into its dark waters. When questioned she had no explanation. Finally one night the husband awoke to a strange cry, the wife was not in her bed, the nurse was sent to fetch the child, but she was not in her crib. They searched the house and eventually found the baby floating in the water of the well. *(Beat)* The woman was found nearby inconsolable, and was, a few days later, discovered drowned at the bottom of the well herself.

GIRL: That's so sad.

MARCÉ: What can we infer from these observations?

GIRL: That having a baby is not always good for your brain?

MARCÉ: *(Smiling at her)* Little girl, you have the mind of a scientist.

(As he hands her the peanut plants The GIRL *beams back at him. They finish packing up experiment.)*

*(*SUSAN *has turned away from them, rocking resolutely in the chair)*

(Fade to next scene)

Scene Fourteen

*(*DAVID *stands at the door, with his laptop overcoat, and plane tickets.* SUSAN *sits in the rocker, rocking, calmly, holding the baby.* GRANDMA, *the* GIRL *and* MARCÉ *gather behind her.)*

DAVID: I left my itinerary on the fridge. The number for the hotel is on it, but if you need to reach me use the cell. I'll call you as soon as I check in. She's asleep now, why don't you use this time to do something for yourself.

SUSAN: Okay.

VOICE: Why don't you just kill yourself and get it over with. Go go get the knife out of the drawer and just get it over with...

DAVID: You're gonna be alright, Suze, really, you're a great mother. I see it even if you don't. You just gotta hang in there and you'll be fine.

SUSAN: I know.

DAVID: *(He puts down his stuff and embraces her)* Promise me if things get bad, you'll call Terri.

SUSAN: Okay.

VOICE: Bad mother bad mother you really are hopeless do you think you are fooling everyone, maybe you can fool everyone but you know the truth, how stupid you are, how needy, how afraid.

DAVID: Look she's sleeping, why don't you put on some music, and go take a long hot bath. Write in your journal, or just sleep, she should be down for an hour, you go down for an hour.

SUSAN: Okay.

DAVID: The fridge is stocked, you got all the formula you'll need, diapers. You should be good till I get back. You won't have to go to the store for anything, but promise me you'll get out - go for a walk or something everyday, a little bit. Go to the library, they have story time for babies. Why don't you do that?

SUSAN: I will.

DAVID: I better go, the sooner I go, the sooner I'll be back. I love you. Hang in there. *(Beat, voice over) Au revoir.*

SUSAN: *(Hesitates) Au revoir.*

Scene Fifteen

(A week later. SUSAN looks disheveled, unbathed. She is "multitasking" between several different things at once, completing none of them, when the baby starts to cry. She suddenly realizes she doesn't know where the baby is. She tears everything apart searching frantically, before finding baby in a drawer. Then the phone rings. She nearly goes flying over a chair, as she lunges for the phone as if it were a life preserver.)

SUSAN: Hello... *(She continues pacing through the house)* Oh, David, oh my god, thank god it's you. I did what you said, I took her out, for a walk to the library. I was fooled at first, lulled into thinking everything would be

all right. So proud of myself walking down the street,
hey, look at me, I'm pushing a stroller. I'd gotten her in
her snowsuit, and outside, we're going to the library
like any other normal mother and her child. And then
I got there. What were you thinking? *(Beat)* I took her to
the library, like you said, the library and I swear to god,
the janitor, the cleaning guy, he was going to take us all
hostage. He'd locked the door, he said by mistake and I
never noticed before he was an Arab I thought he was
African American, but he isn't. And have you noticed
there are more of them. They are on every street corner,
talking on cell phones, coming out of apartment
buildings, driving by in old honda's with
Massachussetts license plates, with video cameras,
David—the janitor in the library. He's strange, you
have to admit, the way he looks at you, like he knows
you suspect him, like he's *guilty* already. That's the way
a *terrorist* looks and don't tell me I don't know, I saw it
in his eyes and I don't trust him and not with a baby for
godsake and I'm standing there, shocked speechless the
door was locked and he had locked it and I'm thinking,
I have nothing to feed this baby with, she's going to get
hungry and she's going to start screaming and you
know how she is she doesn't stop until you feed her
and I had no *bottle with me,* first of all what the fuck
is wrong with me that I go out for a two hour walk
with no fucking bottle, not even a goddamn pacifier
I deserve *everything* everything I get,I told that doctor
and she wouldn't believe me, she said try the soy as if
that was the answer to all my problems well I tried the
soy drank it myself in fact and almost threw up it was
awful because its nothing but chemicals, chemical soup,
so we won't even get into that conversation since I
already told you what kind of half-assed retarded
mother I am. *What?* What? *(Brief pause)* You don't
understand. We live in a Jewish neighborhood. I know
we're not Jewish but that's where we live, you can't tell

me they don't have a plot to blow up Jewish
neighborhoods. Then why do they have policemen
everywhere? I might be crazy but I'm not blind.
It doesn't matter. They've already won. Because even if
they don't commit the act, there are imaginary random
acts of terror going on in my brain *every day*. Yes, I think
about it everyday David, don't you? When you walk on
that plane tomorrow, or tomorrow or whenever the hell
it is you are coming home I thought you were coming
home a year ago, you are coming home tomorrow
aren't you? I told you ten days would be too long,
it was too long David, too long. I just got pushed over
the brink I am hanging on by my fingernails because
I love her so much and I know how dangerous it is to
have me as her mother— I see you staring at me behind
that chair. I don't know if I can survive this David, it is
too profound, it is too much painful animal love I had
no idea how gut-wrenching this would be. No, there
is nobody else here, don't be jealous, I know how I've
neglected you these last months, but it's nobody's fault
but your own you wouldn't listen like somebody else
is listening. Look at her how she has no idea how close
she came to not being here today, if that janitor decided
to go and do it, her head if you could see it is snuggled
under my breasts and she's listening to my heartbeat as
if I am the world and my breath is the ocean, my voice
the stars, my hands the air and she is so trusting that
nothing will ever hurt her, and it is a *lie David a big fat
lie*; when I see her like this I try to communicate to her
how much I love her and that I will try oh god I am so
sorry I will try to protect her no matter how I feel about
it, I would kill with my nails and teeth the first thing
that would come near her including you buddy,
including me, especially including me, so come home
or don't come home but don't say I didn't warn you,
because it is *red alert now David, red alert*! (*Slams down the
receiver. Looking around for* GIRL) Now you get your ass

out from behind that couch or wherever the hell you are right now.

(GIRL *comes out from behind the chair, holding the monitor behind her back*)

SUSAN: Don't you know I know where you are at all times and it's impossible to spy on me?!

(*Phone starts ringing; baby starts crying.*)

GIRL: Why don't you put the baby in the crib and take a nap.

SUSAN: *I can't sleep you know that.* I haven't slept in days. In weeks. Sleep has been broken.

(GIRL *holds out monitor*)

GIRL: If you don't put the baby down I am going to turn this on.

SUSAN: I think you need a bath.

GIRL: You're the one.

(*Switches on monitor, static*)

SUSAN: Oh yes, I need a bath, I've been puked on and shit on and spat on and yes, there is *babyshit* in my *hair* the color of gold because I am Rapunzel Goddamnit trapped in her tower except nobody is coming to climb these *golden tresses*!

(*She is going after* GIRL, *knocking furniture and things out of the way*)

GIRL: You're taking it out on me! I didn't do anything!

(SUSAN *grabs a fistful of* GIRL's *hair and starts to drag her to bathtub, we hear water running loud.*)

SUSAN: You're just filthy dirty and you're getting in this tub and washed once and for all!

(SUSAN pushes the GIRL head first into the water, the GIRL fights to come up. Water splashing, SUSAN pushes the GIRL under the water again. Again the GIRL resists.)

GIRL: I didn't ask to be born either!

(This stops her. SUSAN lets her go.)

SUSAN: No you didn't, and neither did she. So what do we do about it. Maybe we should just stop the bullshit now and end it.

(GIRL freezes, SUSAN leaves tub with water running and walks over to bassinet, staring down at baby. The monitor echoes what SUSAN says next.)

SUSAN: I could save you so much grief.

(The phone is still ringing.)

GIRL: Answer it.

(SUSAN doesn't move.)

GIRL: Answer.

(SUSAN is still staring omninously at baby.)

(GIRL picks up receiver and hands it to SUSAN who doesn't move. She starts shouting helplessly toward receiver as she holds it out to SUSAN.)

GIRL: *Come home! Come home!!*

(SUSAN takes the phone.)

GIRL: *(Whispers)* Please come home.

(SUSAN gently puts the phone back in the cradle. The sound of water roars on.)

(Black out)

Scene Sixteen

(SUSAN *sits on the edge of the tub, she holds the baby in a towel, she is soaked from head to foot. The* GIRL *sits opposite her, also soaked. They rock slightly back and forth, a mirror image.*)

SUSAN: I'm sorry.

GIRL: I know.

SUSAN: I had to.

GIRL: I know.

SUSAN: I never mean to hurt you.

GIRL: I know.

SUSAN: Or the baby. (*Silence, rocking*) Do you forgive me?

GIRL: I'm still here aren't I? (*Rocking, silence*) I'll always be here.

SUSAN: I know. (*Rocking/silence*) When I was pregnant I had this dream I thought meant I was entering the community of Mothers. So I took it to be a good omen. The pool was crystal clear, but it was really an ocean, full of the women I am connected to, but never knew. My mother. My Grandmother. Her Mother. Her Mother. Her mother. Her mother. (*Rocking*) But none of them were looking at me. I entered the water and that's when all my troubles began. The water was clear, but my mind became cloudy. I don't want her to have to join that pool of women sitting in still water waiting for the tsunami to come. Because it's coming. The dream was some kind of warning. Because if it was a welcoming, I think the women in the water would have been looking at me. Don't you? Looking at me, smiling warm motherly smiles. But they were all turned away.

Their faces blank. Lost in their own disconnection.
Like my mother. The message is, has always been:
Honey you are on your own now: sink or swim, sink or
swim, sink, swim, sink, swim. *(Stops rocking)* She's cold.
Why don't you hold her?

(GIRL *takes baby*)

SUSAN: You should have been the mother. You have
been the better mother all along. *(She gets up, looks at
baby. Whispers)* My little peanut, my little fish, my heart.
Forgive me.

(MARCÉ *enters waiting for* SUSAN. *She walks towards
him as he speaks to her in French, this time she seems to
understand him.* GIRL *takes her place rocking the baby*)

MARCÉ: *Venez, Madame, vous devez maintenant aller
dormir. Au réveil, vous verrez tout plus clairement, et vous
devrez fair face. [Come Madame, you will go to sleep now.
After sleep you will see everything more clearly, and then
will come the hard part.]*

(SUSAN *exits with* MARCÉ. *The* GIRL *remains sitting on the
tub, holding baby.*)

GIRL: *(Rocking)* Goodnight, sweet baby.

(Fade to black on GIRL *rocking.)*

END OF PLAY

English translation, page 3

MARCÉ: *Bonjour Madame.* How are you feeling? You don't have to say a word. Lay back. You have worked very hard this evening. Let yourself rest while you can.

SUSAN: I left the water running in the sink.

MARCÉ: *(Frowning slightly, touches her forehead clucks his tongue)* slight fever, sticky sweat covers the face, the face is pale, puffed, the expression, stunned, the pulse is fast, say ahh, *(He sticks his tongue out, she imitates him)* the tongue is coated. May I? *(He begins to palpate her uterus.)* The uterus is enlarged, it is tender, yes, but it will heal. I recommend sleep. And long warm baths, time will take care of the rest. Is there someone to tell you to be gentle with yourself?

SUSAN: I don't speak french.

MARCÉ: *(In heavily accented English)* We must ask the question: what is the connection between the uterus and the mind?

www.ingramcontent.com/pod-product-compliance
Lightning Source LLC
Chambersburg PA
CBHW070025110426
42741CB00034B/2569